# LEGENDARY LANDFORMS
# CANYONS

by Rebecca Pettiford

# Ideas for Parents and Teachers

Pogo Books let children practice reading informational text while introducing them to nonfiction features such as headings, labels, sidebars, maps, and diagrams, as well as a table of contents, glossary, and index.

Carefully leveled text with a strong photo match offers early fluent readers the support they need to succeed.

## Before Reading

- "Walk" through the book and point out the various nonfiction features. Ask the student what purpose each feature serves.
- Look at the glossary together. Read and discuss the words.

## Read the Book

- Have the child read the book independently.
- Invite him or her to list questions that arise from reading.

## After Reading

- Discuss the child's questions. Talk about how he or she might find answers to those questions.
- Prompt the child to think more. Ask: Have you ever seen a canyon? Where was it? How big was it?

Pogo Books are published by Jump!
5357 Penn Avenue South
Minneapolis, MN 55419
www.jumplibrary.com

Library of Congress Cataloging-in-Publication Data

Names: Pettiford, Rebecca, author.
Title: Canyons / by Rebecca Pettiford.
Description: Minneapolis, MN: Jump!, Inc., [2017]
Series: Legendary landforms | "Pogo Books are published by Jump!." | Audience: Ages 7-10.
Includes bibliographical references and index.
Identifiers: LCCN 2016045761 (print)
LCCN 2016047840 (ebook) | ISBN 9781620317068 (hardcover: alk. paper) | ISBN 9781620317440 (pbk.)
ISBN 9781624965838 (ebook)
Subjects: LCSH: Canyons—Juvenile literature.
Landforms—Juvenile literature.
Classification: LCC GB561 .P477 2017 (print)
LCC GB561 (ebook) | DDC 551.44/2—dc23
LC record available at https://lccn.loc.gov/2016045761

Editor: Kirsten Chang
Book Designer: Leah Sanders
Photo Researcher: Leah Sanders

Photo Credits: Galyna Andrushko/Shutterstock, cover; Yobro10/Thinkstock, 1; Jane Rix/Shutterstock, 3; Marek Zuk/Alamy, 4; GuilhermeMesquita/Shutterstock, 5; Danita Delimont/Getty, 6-7; beboy/Shutterstock, 8-9; Sergey Novikov/Shutterstock, 10-11; Alex Mustard/Getty, 12-13; Anton Foltin/Shutterstock, 14; LordRunar/iStock, 15; bukki88/Thinkstock, 16-17; Bill Hatcher/Getty, 18-19; David Wall Photo/Getty, 20-21; Demetrio Carrasco/Getty, 23.

Printed in the United States of America at Corporate Graphics in North Mankato, Minnesota.

# TABLE OF CONTENTS

# CHAPTER 1

## A CRACK IN THE EARTH

Have you ever been in a **canyon**? They are deep and narrow. Steep rock walls rise from the ground.

Did you know these huge **landforms** are created by wind and water? Let's find out how!

**Erosion** creates canyons. Water and wind remove **sediment** such as stones and sand. This creates a path that deepens over time. It forms a canyon or **gorge**.

## DID YOU KNOW?

People cause erosion, too. How? We mine. We build. We garden. This weakens **topsoil**. It wears away.

# CHAPTER 2

## CARVING A CANYON

A canyon begins when a river flows through dry land.

Over millions of years, the river cuts away layers of rock. It lowers a canyon's floor. It widens its walls. Rivers still shape canyons today.

In some cases, floods form canyons. Flash floods fill cracks in desert rock. Rushing water washes away sediment. Narrow **slot canyons** form. They are deeper than they are wide. The walls are high and smooth.

Even the ocean has canyons. They are called submarine canyons. Underwater **currents** cut them into the ocean floor.

## DID YOU KNOW?

One of the largest canyons isn't on Earth. It's on Mars! It is 1,864 miles (3,000 kilometers) long. It is 372 miles (600 km) wide and five miles (8 km) deep.

# CHAPTER 3

## THE GRAND CANYON

The Grand Canyon is one of the most famous canyons on Earth. It is in northern Arizona. The Colorado River formed it. It took about six million years.

The Grand Canyon cuts through the Colorado Plateau. This **plateau** formed millions of years ago. A part of Earth's **crust** rose higher than the land around it. This was due to **tectonic** activity.

The Grand Canyon is the biggest canyon in North America. It is 277 miles (446 km) long and 18 miles (29 km) wide. It is over a mile (1.6 km) deep. That is about as tall as four Empire State Buildings!

Empire State
Building

**Geologists** study the Grand Canyon. They learn how the land changed over time. The rock layers show what the weather was like at different times. Dry years show up as thin layers.

Canyons are also good places to study **fossils**. Fossils are preserved well in hot, dry areas.

## DID YOU KNOW?

Fossils of scorpion and centipede footprints were found at the Grand Canyon. No dinosaur fossils have been found, though. Why? The canyon rocks are older than dinosaurs!

Rock layers help predict how the landform will change. Scientists think the Grand Canyon gets deeper by one foot (0.3 meters) every 200 years. They say it will deepen as long as the Colorado River flows.

Millions of people visit the Grand Canyon each year. Do you want to see this legendary landform? You can hike trails, ride mules, and enjoy the view.

# ACTIVITIES & TOOLS

## EROSION AT WORK

In this activity, you will make a small landform. You will learn how water erodes it.

**What You Need:**
- 2 cups sand
- 2 cups dirt
- small stones (about a handful)
- a large shallow pan
- eyedropper or baster
- watering can filled with water
- pencil and paper

❶ At one end of the pan, mix the sand, dirt, and stones with some water. Add enough water so that you can shape it into a small landform. You can let it dry overnight if it is too wet.

❷ Use the eyedropper or baster to squeeze a few drops of water on your landform. What happened? Write it down.

❸ Get your watering can. Pour some "heavy rain" on your landform. What happened? Write it down.

❹ Pour out some water from the can's wide opening to flood your landform. What happened? You will notice that each time you added more water, more sediment (sand, stones, dirt) washed away. This is how erosion forms canyons!

# GLOSSARY

**canyon:** A deep, narrow landform that is shaped by running water and other natural forces.

**crust:** The outer layer of Earth.

**currents:** Continuous movements of water in a body of water.

**erosion:** The slow destruction of something by water and wind.

**fossils:** The remains or imprints of ancient life.

**geologists:** Scientists who study the history of the earth, especially as recorded in rocks.

**gorge:** A deep, narrow valley with steep sides.

**landforms:** Natural features of Earth's surface.

**plateau:** A broad, flat area of high land.

**sediment:** Material such as stones and sand deposited by water, wind, or glaciers.

**slot canyons:** Narrow canyons formed by water rushing through rock; a slot canyon is deeper than it is wide.

**tectonic:** Relating to changes in the structure of Earth's surface.

**topsoil:** The top layer of soil.

# INDEX

# TO LEARN MORE

**Learning more is as easy as 1, 2, 3.**

1) **Go to www.factsurfer.com**

2) **Enter "legendarycanyons" into the search box.**

3) **Click the "Surf" button to see a list of websites.**

With factsurfer, finding more information is just a click away.